REDMOND
O'HANLON

A RIVER IN BORNEO

PENGUIN BOOKS

PENGUIN BOOKS

Published by the Penguin Group. Penguin Books Ltd, 27 Wrights Lane, London w8 5TZ, England. Penguin Books USA Inc., 375 Hudson Street, New York, New York 10014, USA. Penguin Books Australia Ltd, Ringwood, Victoria, Australia. Penguin Books Canada Ltd, 10 Alcorn Avenue, Toronto, Ontario, Canada M4V 3B2. Penguin Books (NZ) Ltd, 182–190 Wairau Road, Auckland 10, New Zealand · Penguin Books Ltd, Registered Offices: Harmondsworth, Middlesex, England · These extracts are from *Into the Heart of Borneo*, by Redmond O'Hanlon, published in Penguin Books 1985. This edition published 1996. Copyright © Redmond O'Hanlon 1984. All rights reserved · Typeset by Rowland Phototypesetting Ltd, Bury St Edmunds, Suffolk · Printed in England by Clays Ltd, St Ives plc · Except in the United States of America, this book is sold subject to the condition that it shall not, by way of trade or otherwise, be lent, re-sold, hired out, or otherwise circulated without the publisher's prior consent in any form of binding or cover other than that in which it is published and without a similar condition including this condition being imposed on the subsequent purchaser · 10 9 8 7 6 5 4 3 2 1

In the last Sea Dyak longhouse upstream on the Baleh river, Rumah Pengulu-Jimbun, were a great many skulls hanging in rattan nets from the cross-beams of the gallery roof. I inspected them carefully. The teeth had been worn almost uniformly flat, and there were no fillings, which was comforting. Each one was busily tenanted, not by brains, but by digger wasps. Too large to crawl in by the optic nerve holes behind the eye-sockets, the insects had made their entrances at the base of the crania, where the heads had been severed from their spinal columns.

'Very old,' said Leon, our tracker and interpreter, who was good at guessing one's thoughts at such moments. 'Maybe some belong Japanese.'

'Come on – surely just a little head-hunting still goes on?' I asked. 'Every now and then when no one is looking?'

'No, no – absolute no. But if,' said Leon with one of his big brown grins, 'if we find someone we don't like, not one bit, all alone in the jungle, then that's called murder; and that's quite different. And then it would be a waste not to take his head, wouldn't it?'

'But you took a lot of Japanese heads, didn't you?' I said, thinking of Tom Harrison's ten-bob-a-nob campaign in the war.

'Every one of them, all of them,' said Leon with great serious-ness. 'You ask the old men, you ask Dana. Just around that far

1

bend in the river, by the rapids beyond the islands, one of the great battles in the Second World War took place. There were eight Japanese, all armed with guns, coming up in a boat they'd stolen from us. And we had two hundred warriors from here with their spears and blowpipes hidden on the left bank, and two hundred warriors from two different longhouses hidden on the right bank, and they killed all the Japanese. And so there were eight heads, but there were three chiefs, and so they fought because they couldn't divide them equally. You know about the Second World War?'

'Just a bit,' I said.

'Well – one party of Japanese came to Borneo to take our padi. And one party stayed at home. And the Japanese were so cruel to the Iban that the English couldn't bear it. So they came to help us. But there weren't enough English to kill all the Japanese in both places, so they asked the Americans to help. So the Americans bombed the longhouses at Hiroshima and Nagasaki and the English helped us to take all the heads of all the Japanese in Borneo and that was the end of the Second World War.'

'And a good thing too,' I said.

An old man (old for Borneo), apparently blind, sitting in the shade on the split-bamboo floor, attacked by some disease which had destroyed the pigment in his cells and left him blotched with white, nodded.

At midday, waving goodbye to the chief and to the thirty or forty children and the thirty or forty dogs which had gathered on the bank, we climbed into our dugout canoe and set off upriver towards the interior, where neither Dana, nor Leon nor Inghai (our youngest tracker and our bow look-out) had ever been. For us, the unknown had begun at the coast, at the delta of the great river Rajang; for them, the unknown began now.

After about ten miles the hill-padi fields of Rumah Pengulu-Jimbun gave way to well-established secondary forest, ground whose vegetation had not been slashed and burned and cleared for a one-year's crop of rice for fifty years or so; and then the primeval jungle began. The river seemed to close in on us: the two-hundred-foot-high trees crowded down the slopes of the hills, almost to the water's edge, an apparently endless chaos of different species of tree, every kind of green, even under the uniform glare of a tropical sun; parasitic growths sprouted everywhere, ferns fanned out from every angle in the branches, creepers as thick as legs gripped each other and tangled down to the surface of the water, their tips twining down in the current like river-weed.

The river itself began to turn and twist, too, the banks behind us appearing to merge together into one vast and impenetrable thicket, shutting us in from behind just as the trees ahead stepped aside a meagre pace or two to let the river swirl down ahead. The outboard motor, manned by Leon and set on a special wooden frame at the stern of the canoe, pushed us past foaming little tributaries, islets, shingle banks strewn with huge rounded boulders, half-hidden coves scooped round by whirlpools. Way above the last of the logging camps whose bulldozed topsoil, falling into the water, turns the lower reaches of the rivers of Borneo brown, here the Baleh was clear, deep green from the reflection of the trees. We really were voyaging upriver – at first I thought it an optical illusion, but the canoe was actually climbing up a volume of water great enough to sustain an almost constant angle of ascent, even on the stretches of water between the jagged steps of the rapids.

Spits of land had formed wherever smaller streams joined the main flow, and here driftwood was piled, stacks of hardwood planed smooth by the rush of floodwater, flung together, bleached grey by the sun. We stopped by one such pile to hide a drum of petrol. A monitor lizard, reared up on its front legs, watched us for a moment with its dinosauric eyes and then scuttled away between the broken branches. A Brahminy kite, flying low enough for us to hear the rush of air through the primary feathers of its wings, circled overhead watching us, its flecked-brown belly white in the sun, before it soared away, mewing its shrill call like a buzzard.

Further up, the rapids began to become more numerous and more turbulent and, at each one, as Leon drove the canoe for the central cascade of the current at full power whilst Dana and Inghai, their back muscles bunched, poled the bow to the left or the right of each oncoming rock, heavy waves of water would crash over and into the boat. James Fenton, sitting opposite me on the duckboards in the centre of the canoe and facing upstream, was reading his way through Pat Rogers's new edition of the complete poems of Swift, a straw boater on his bald head, his white shirt buttoned at the neck and at the wrists.

'Some of this juvenilia is pretty feeble,' James would mutter, displeased.

'Quite so. But – er – James?'

'Yes?'

'Rapid 583/2, Green Heave Strength six-out-of-ten, is approaching.'

With a second or two to spare, James would shut his book, mark his place in it with a twig, slip it neatly under an edge of the tarpaulin, place his left buttock upon it, shut his eyes, get drenched, open his eyes, squeeze the water from his beard with his right hand, retrieve his book and carry on reading.

Every five hundred yards or so, a Lesser fish-eagle would regard us with its yellow eye, motionless at first, its grey feet clamped to a favourite branch overhanging the edge of the river, flying off only as we drew almost level, flapping gently just ahead of the canoe to the limit of its territory, and then doubling back. There were Greyheaded fish-eagles, too, larger and more sluggish, the base of their tails white rather than grey-brown. It was odd to be journeying like this, preceded by eagles.

The first real sight of the Borneo kingfishers was equally startling. Brighter than any illustration could ever be, apparently radiating blue and orange from its back and stomach all around itself into the background of green until it seemed to be a bird four times its size, its large bill translucent, carmine-red in the sun, the Black-capped kingfisher (in fact an eater of insects) was often so tame it never bothered to fly from us at all, but sat bobbing on its bough, *chick-chicking* loud and shrill, furious to be disturbed. The Stork-billed kingfisher, however, much bigger, its front end built like the nose-cone of a missile, always flew off, screaming as it went, the silky light blue of its rump disappearing fast and low upriver to a hiding perch in some habitual tree.

A small heron, the Little green heron, slate-grey and furtive, skulked about the river margins, or the island shingle banks, or amongst the beached driftwood; and our own Common sandpiper, always solitary (except at dusk when we might see three or four come skimming past just above the water) seemed to like riding on drifting logs, hopping off to run about the mud or the shingle. 5

Looking at one, as small and brown, as agile and elegant and friendly as if I had been watching it in Poole Harbour, I thought of Beccari's record of one of its feeding habits: 'When crocodiles lie thus with open jaws, small shore birds, especially waders of the sandpiper kind, which are always running about on the banks in search of food, enter the huge reptiles' mouths to capture any such small fry as may have sought refuge among the teeth or in the folds of the mucous membrane of the mouth or pharynx. Indeed, if I remember right, I have witnessed the thing myself; but now as I write I cannot feel quite sure that it was not one of many stories told me by my men.'

James, his huge head laid back on the hump of our kit under the tarpaulin, was having one of his five-minute snoozes. The vein on his right temple was distended with blood, a sure sign that his cerebellum was awash with extra dissolved oxygen, and that some piece of programming, vital to the production of a future poem, was in progress.

'James!'

An eye opened.

'What is it?'

'Just this – if you *do* see a log floating *upriver*, let me know.'

'Crocodiles?'

'Well, not the estuarine one that really goes for you. Not up here. But Tweedie and Harrison think we might see the freshwater Gharial. The fifteen-foot one with the five-foot snout and all those teeth.'

'Really Redmond,' said James, raising himself up on an elbow and looking about, 'you're absurd. You live in the nineteenth century. Everything's changed, although you don't appear to notice.

Nowadays you will have no difficulty whatever in recognizing a crocodile. Everyone knows – they come with an outboard motor at the back and a Kenwood mixer at the front.'

I sat back in the boat. When the temperature is 110°F and the humidity 98 per cent, when you're soaking wet and rotting a bit in the crutch, then even weak jokes like that, in the worst possible taste, seem extraordinarily funny.

At five o'clock in the afternoon we entered a wider stretch of river where a tributary joined the main stream and a low ridge of shingle had formed down the centre of the water course. Dana decided to make camp.

'Good fishing. Very good,' said Leon, looking at the swirling white water, the fallen trees and the eddies by the far bank.

We pulled the canoe well out of the water and tied its bow-rope high up the trunk of a tree, in case of floods in the night, and then stretched out on the sand for a rest. Butterflies began to gather. Hundreds of butterflies, flying at different heights and speeds, floating, flapping awkwardly in small bursts, gliding, fluttering like bats, winnowing, some flying fast and direct like a wren in trouble, made their way towards us and settled on our boots and trousers, clustered on our shirts, sucked the sweat from our arms. There were Whites, Yellows and Blues; Swallow-tails, black, banded or spotted with blue-greens; and, just outside the clustering circle of small butterflies, the magnificent species which Alfred Russel Wallace named after James Brooke, *Troides brookeana*, the Rajah Brooke's birdwing.

Sucking our clothes and skin with their thread-like proboscides at one end, the butterflies exuded a white goo over us from their anal vents at the other. Getting up, brushing them off as gently as possible, I walked away from my companion the mandatory few yards and took a pee myself. Whilst my patch of urine was still steaming slightly on the muddy sand, the males of Rajah Brooke's birdwing (the females, fully employed laying eggs in the jungle trees, are seldom seen) flew over and crowded down on it, elbowing each other with the joints on their legs, pushing and shoving to get at the liquid, the brilliant green feather-shaped marks on their black wings trembling slightly as they fed. I began, prematurely, to feel a part of things.

In fact, having run to the canoe to fetch the shockproof, waterproof, more-or-less-everything-proof (but, sadly, fixed-lens) heavy-duty Fuji cameras, I began to feel, as I crawled on my stomach towards the pullulating insects, more than a passing pride in the quality of my offering. After all, some thirteen inches from my own nose and closing, was the very butterfly which Wallace described in 1855:

the *Ornithoptera brookeana*, one of the most elegant species known. This beautiful creature has very long and pointed wings, almost resembling a sphinx moth in shape. It is deep velvety black, with a curved band of spots of a brilliant metallic-green colour extending across the wings from tip to tip, each spot being shaped exactly like a small triangular feather, and having very much the effect of a row of the Wing Coverts of the Mexican trojon laid upon black velvet. The only other marks are a broad neck-collar of vivid crimson, and a few delicate white touches on the outer margins of the hind wings. This species, which was then quite new and which I named after Sir James Brooke, was very rare. It was seen occasionally flying swiftly in the clearings, and now and then settling for an instant at puddles and muddy places, so that I only succeeded in capturing two or three specimens.

While photographing this butterfly (with a fixed wide-angle lens which I knew would produce a hopeless picture), which later proved to be very common all the way up the Baleh to its source, I felt the excitement that Wallace himself describes, on capturing its close cousin *Ornithoptera croesus*:

Fine specimens of the male are more than seven inches across the wings, which are velvety black and fiery orange, the latter colour replacing the green of the allied species. The beauty and brilliancy of this insect are indescribable, and none but a naturalist can understand the intense excitement I experienced when I at length captured it . . . my heart began to beat violently, the blood rushed to my head, and I felt much more like fainting than I have done when in apprehension of immediate death. I had a headache the rest of the day, so great was the excitement produced by what will appear to most people a very inadequate cause.

I, too, had a headache for the rest of the day, but then perhaps it was the sun, or the mere thought of our fishing equipment. For after a burning swig all round from the *arak* rice-brandy five-gallon converted petrol can, Dana, Leon and Inghai, drawing their *parangs* from their carved wooden scabbards, set off to cut down the saplings for our pole-beds; and I decided it was time that James and I taught them how to fish to maximum effect, like Englishmen. But first a little practice would be necessary.

Withdrawing quietly behind a massive jumble of boulders, well out of sight, I unpacked our precious cargo. Two new extendable rods, the toughest in town. A hundred yards of heavy line. A heavy bag of assorted lead weights. A termite's nest of swivels. A thornbush of hooks. Fifty different spinners, their spoons flashing in the sun, all shapes and all sizes for every kind of fish in every sort of inland water.

'The trouble is,' said James, flicking a rod handle and watching the sections telescope out into the blue beyond, 'my elder brother was the fisherman. That was his thing, you see, he filled that role. So I had to pretend it was a bore; and I never learned.'

'What? You never fished?'

'No. Never. What about you?'

'Well, *my* elder brother went fishing.'

'So you can't either?'

'Not exactly. Not with a rod. I used to go mackerel fishing with a line. All over the place.'

'Mackerel fishing! Now you tell me!' said James, looking really quite agitated and frightening a bright orange damsel-fly off his hat. 'Still,' he said, calming down, 'if *they* could do it it can't be that diffy, can it?'

'Of course not – you just stick the spinner and swivels and weights on that end and swing it through the air.'

The heat was unbearable. The fiddling was insupportable. The gut got tangled; the hooks stuck in our fingers; the knot diagram would have given Baden-Powell a blood clot in the brain. We did it all and forgot the nasty little weights. But eventually we were ready to kill fish.

'The SAS say it's simpler to stick in a hand-grenade.'

'They're right,' said James.

'But the Major said all you had to do was hang your dick in the water and pull it out with fish on it.'

'Why don't you stick your dick in the river?' said James.

Standing firm and straight, James cast the spinner into the river. It landed in the water straight down at the end of the rod. Clunk. James pulled. The line snapped. We went through the whole nasty rigmarole again, with fresh swivels, weights and spinner.

'Try again. Throw it a little further.'

James reached right back and then swung the rod forwards and sideways as if he was axeing a tree.

At that very moment, it seemed, the Borneo banded hornet, *Vesta tropica*, sank its sting into my right buttock.

'Jesus!' I said.

It was huge and jointed, this hornet, flashing red and silver in the sun.

'You are hooked up,' said James, matter-of-factly. 'You have a spinner in your bum.'

There was a weird, gurgling, jungle-sound behind us. Dana, Leon and Inghai were leaning against the boulders. The Iban, when they decide that something is really funny, and know that they are going to laugh for a long time, lie down first.

Dana, Leon and Inghai lay down.

'You should try it with harpoon!' shrieked Leon, helpless.

With great ceremony we presented our rods to Dana and Leon and a compensatory extra helping of weights and spinners to little Inghai. And with equal aplomb, the Iban took the useless gifts into care, wrapped them in cloth, and placed them in the bottom of the canoe.

Our beds had been expertly set up: two poles run through the specially designed tubes of the SAS tarpaulins to form a stretcher, itself supported on a rectangular frame, a four-poster, lashed together with rattan strips and awaiting only a mosquito net and a cover. Tying the net and the canvas roof to the surrounding trees with parachute cord, a small bed-length of insect-free security emerged in the jungle. Campaign-proved, everything fitted, tied together, overlapped, held fast.

Dana and Leon had almost finished building their own shelter. Having constructed a platform of poles about two feet off the jungle floor, they were laying a lattice-work of branches to make a sloping roof. Inghai returned from the hillside with bundles of enormous palm leaves, and the structure was complete. Lying inside on a leaf-bed, one's feet towards the four-foot opening overlooking the river, the roof coming down at a bright green angle tight above one's head, it seemed the childhood tree-house *par excellence*.

Dana then began to build his own little house. Six-foot tall, two-feet square, with a conventional triangular roof and a small platform halfway up, its use was not apparent. For the spirits? For heads that might saunter by?

'For fish,' said Leon, 'for smoking fish. Now we show you how to fish like the Iban.'

Taking their wooden harpoons from the canoe, Leon and Inghai dived into the river; and disappeared completely, like a pair of Great crested grebe. A full forty seconds later they bobbed up again, right over on the far bank. Leon stood up and held an enormous fish above his head, harpooned through the flank. Inghai, as befitted his size, held up a tiddler. Much yelling in Iban took place. Dana, evidently stung into action, took a large weighted net out of the canoe, a *jala*, and made his way upstream to the shingle bank. Swinging it back and forth in both hands, swaying slightly, he cast it out; a slowly spinning circle of white mesh settled on the water, and sank. Jumping in, scrabbling about to collect the bottom ends of the net, Dana finally scooped it all up again, together with three catfish. They looked at us lugubriously, an immensely long whisker or barbel, their feelers, drooping down from either side of their mouths. Dana detached them with the greatest care, avoiding their dorsal and pectoral spines which, presumably, were poisonous, and tossed them up the shingle.

Leon and Inghai returned with six fish, all of the same species, sebarau, handsome, streamlined, and, unlike the smooth and mucus-covered catfish, armoured with large silver scales and adorned with a bold black bar down each side.

Inghai collected driftwood and made two fires, one on the beach and the other at the base of the smoking-house. Leon gutted the fish, cut them into sections, placed some in a salting tin, some on the smoking-rack, and some in a water-filled cooking pot. Two ancient cauldrons, slung from a high wooden frame, bubbled over the fire: one full of fish pieces and one full of sticky rice. Dana, having set a larger net part-across the current, supported by ropes to an overhanging branch and by white polystyrene floats, returned for supper.

Dusk came suddenly, and, equally suddenly, Eared nightjars appeared, hawking insects, stooping and turning in their haphazard, bat-like way, along the tops of the trees above the river banks, seeming half-transparent and weightless in their ghostly agility, like falcons weirdly deprived of their power and strike and push. And they were whistling to each other.

After about ten minutes, they vanished. Which was just as well, because it had dawned on me that the fish and rice in my mess-tin would need all the attention I could give it. The sebarau was tasteless, which did not matter, and full of bones, which did. It was like a hair-brush caked in lard. James had made the same discovery.

'Redmond, don't worry,' he whispered, 'if you need a tracheotomy I have a biro-tube in my baggage.'

It was time to go to bed. We washed our mess-tins in the river, kicked out the fire on the beach, and stoked up the smoking-house fire with more wet logs. Slinging my soaking clothes from a tree with parachute cord, I rubbed myself down with a wet towel and, naked, opened my Bergen to pull out my set of dry kit for the night. Every nook and cranny in the bag was alive with inch-long ants. Deciding that anything so huge must be the Elephant ant, and not the Fire ant, which packs a sting like a wasp, I brushed the first wave off my Y-fronts. Glancing up, I was astonished to see my wet clothes swarming with ants, too; a procession of dark ants poured down one side of the rope and up the other, and, all over my wet trousers, hundreds of different moths were feeding. Darkness seemed to rise from the leafy mush of the forest floor; and I rummaged quickly in the outside Bergen pocket for my army torch. As my fingers closed on it, everyone else's little fingers seemed to close on my arm. I drew it out fast and switched on: Elephant ants, this time with massive pincers, were suspended from hand to elbow. The soldiers had arrived. I flicked them off, gratified to hear yelps from James's *basha* as I did so. It was good to know they also went for poets.

Slipping under the mosquito net, I fastened myself into the dark-green camouflage SAS tube. It seemed luxuriously comfortable. You had to sleep straight out like a rifle; but the ants, swarming along the poles, rearing up on their back legs to look for an entry, and the mosquitoes, whining and singing outside the various tunes of their species in black shifting clouds, could not get in.

'Eeeeeee – ai – yack yack yack yack yack!' Something screamed in my ear, with brain-shredding force. And then everyone joined in.

'Eeeeeee – ai – yack yack yack yack yack te yooo!' answered every other giant male cicada, maniacally vibrating the tymbals, drumskin membranes in their cavity amplifiers, the megaphones built into their bodies.

'Shut up!' I shouted.

'Wah wah wah wah wah!' said four thousand frogs.

'Stop it at once!' yelled James.

Clatter-clitter-clatter went our mess-tins over the shingle, being nosed clean by tree shrews.

The Iban laughed. The river grew louder in the darkness. Something hooted. Something screamed in earnest further off. Something shuffled and snuffled around the discarded rice and fish bits flung in a bush from our plates. A porcupine? A civet? A ground squirrel? The long-tailed giant rat? Why not a Clouded leopard? Or, the only really dangerous mammal in Borneo, the long-clawed, short-tempered Sun bear?

I switched off the torch and tried to sleep. But it was no good. The decibel-level was way over the limit allowed in discothèques. And, besides, the fire-flies kept flicking their own torches on and off; and some kind of phosphorescent fungus glowed in the dark like a forty-watt bulb.

I switched on again, clipped the right-angled torch on to my shirt, and settled down for a peaceful read with Hose and McDougall. Discussing the wars of the Kayan, Hose tells us that:

If the defending party should come upon the enemy struggling against a rapid, and especially if the enemy is in difficulties through the upsetting of some of their boats, or in any other way, they may fall upon them in the open bed of the river, and then ensues the comparatively rare event, a stand-up fight in the open. This resolves itself in the main into hand-to-hand duels between pairs of combatants, as in the heroic age. The warriors select their opponents and approach warily; they call upon one another by name, hurling taunts and swaggering boastfully in the heroic style. Each abuses the other's parents, and threatens to use his opponent's skin as a war-coat, or his scrotum as a tobacco-pouch, to take his head and to use his hair as an ornament for a *parang*-handle; or doubt as to the opponent's sex may be insinuated. While this exchange of compliments goes on, the warriors are manoeuvring for favourable positions; each crouches, thrusting forward his left leg, covering himself as completely as possible with his long shield, and dodging to and fro continually. The short javelins and spears are first hurled, and skilfully parried with spear and shield. When a man has expended his stock of javelins and has hurled his spear, he closes in with his *parang*. His enemy seeks to receive the blow of the *parang* on his shield in such a way that the point, entering the wood, may be held fast by it. Feinting and dodging are practised; one man thrusts out his left leg to tempt the other to strike at it and to expose his head in doing so. If one succeeds in catching his enemy's *parang* in his shield, he throws down the shield and dashes upon his now weaponless foe, who takes to his heels, throwing away his shield and relying merely on his swiftness of foot. When one of a pair of combatants is struck down, the other springs upon him and, seizing the long hair of the scalp and yelling in triumph, severs the neck with one or two blows of the *parang*.

It was definitely time to sleep.

At dawn the jungle was half-obscured in a heavy morning mist; and through the cloudy layers of rising moisture came the whooping call, the owl-like, clear, ringing hoot of the female Borneo gibbon.

Replacing the dry socks, pants, trousers and shirt inside two plastic bags inside the damp Bergen, tying them tightly to keep out the ants, I shook the wet clothes. A double-barrelled charge of insects propelled itself from inside my trouser-legs. I groomed my pants free of visible bugs, covered myself in SAS anti-fungus powder until my erogenous zone looked like meat chunks rolled in flour, ready for the heat, and forced my way into clammy battle-dress for the day. It was a nasty five o'clock start; but in half an hour the mist would be gone, the sun merciless, and the river-water soaking one anyway.

Every bush seemed to hold an unseen bird, all in full throat. There were blackbird and thrush, nightingale and warbler-like notes from every side, but more urgent and powerful and relentless, the fortissimo calls of babblers and trillers and bulbuls.

After a breakfast of fish and rice, we re-packed the dugout and set off upriver. The gibbons, having proclaimed the boundaries of their territories, ceased calling. The world changed colour from a dark watery blue to mauve to sepia to pink and then the sun rose, extraordinarily fast.

Inghai put on his peaked cap to shield his eyes from the sun as he sat on the bow and scanned the turbulent water ahead for rocks and logs; Dana, in chiefly style, wore his round hat, as large and intricately patterned as a gaming table; and Leon, proudly switching his outboard to full power, wore a mutant hybrid of pork-pie and homburg. James adjusted his boater, stretched out his legs on his half of the duckboards, and addressed himself to Swift.

Something large and flappy was crossing the river in front of us. Was it a bird disguised as a leaf-skeleton? Was it a day-flying bat disguised as a hair-net? Or was a lattice of tropical worms in

17

transit across my retina? Very slowly, unconcerned, the something made its floating and dipping, floating and dipping, indecisive flight right over the boat: it was an odd idea indeed, *Hestia idea*, a butterfly with grey and white wings like transparent gauze, highly poisonous, and safe from predators. In one of the richest of tropical rain forests, in a natural zone which actually contains more kinds of butterflies and moths than all other habitats of the world put together, it was ridiculously pleasing to have identified just one more species, even if, as I eventually had to admit to James, it was the most immediately obvious of them all.

James, momentarily, re-directed his critical gaze from Swift's sometimes defective scansion, and fixed it upon the surrounding jungle. With AI vision in both eyes which are set so far apart that he does, in this one respect, resemble a hammer-head shark, he announced, in a statement which later became formulaic and, for the Iban (and, well, just a little, for me) the incantation of a shaman of immeasurable age and wisdom summoning the spirits of the forest to dance before him: 'Redmond, I am about to see something *marvellous*.'

The canoe swung into the next bend and there, majestically perched upon a dead branch across an inlet, was a Crested serpent eagle.

'How's that?' said James.

The eagle was thick-set, black and brown and grey, his stomach lightly freckled, his head plumed flat. James was sitting up, boatered, bearded-black, his shirt dazzling white. James looked at the eagle. The eagle looked at James. The eagle, deciding that it was too early in the morning to hallucinate, flapped off into the jungle, puzzled.

Gradually, the rapids became more frequent, more difficult to scale. Leon would align the boat carefully in the deep pools beneath each one, open up to full throttle on a straight run, shut off the engine, cock the propeller well up out of the water as we hit the first curve of white foam, grab his pole as Inghai and Dana snatched up theirs, and then all three would punt the canoe up, in wild rhythm with each other.

They were lean, fit, strong with a lifetime of unremitting exercise, their muscles flexing and bunching, etched out as clearly as Jan van Calcar's illustrations to *De humani corporis fabrica*. But we were about to discover the one disadvantage in their fondly mistaken idea of ourselves, the present misconception in the ancient myth of their oral tradition, that the ancestors of their race had been white, and giants, as strong and courageous, as all-powerful as we, too, must be.

The solid tree-trunk keel of the hollowed-out canoe began to thud against the boulders beneath the cascades of water, lightly at first, and then with alarming violence as the day wore on. We had to jump out beneath each rapid, take the long bow-rope, walk up the stones strewn down beside the fall, wade into the deep current above and pull, guiding the bow up. The water pushed irregularly at our waist and knees, sometimes embracing us like a succubus might (after a year in prison), sometimes trying a flowing rugby tackle, sometimes holding our ankles in a hydrolastic gin-trap; but never entirely friendly. With nothing but locked spines and clamped cartilages we leant back against the great flow of water on its way to the South China Sea, against the forward pull of the rope; itself tugging and slacking as the poled boat broke free or stuck fast.

19

Just in time, by a deep pool, in a harbour formed by two massive fallen hardwoods, Dana ruled that it was noon and we were hungry. The boat was tied up, we collapsed, and Leon went fishing.

Spreading our wet clothes out on the burning hot boulders, James and I took a swim and a wash. The clear shallows were speckled with little fish, darting shoals of orange and silver, weaving flocks of black and red; there were dull-coloured tiddlers, minnow-like, and bright fish with streamers, their small fins fanning in the current; they gathered round our feet, fixed our toes with their tiny eyes, chased whirling flecks of soap in the current.

Dana, intrigued by medicated Vosene, shampooed his glossy black hair and then rinsed it by swimming very fast across the pool underwater, a moving V of ripples on the surface marking his passage through the spins and eddies. Wading ashore, even his dark-blue tattoos glistened in the sun. Covered in circles and rosettes, whorls and lines (soot from a cooking pot, mixed with sweetened water, and punched into the skin with a bamboo stick and small hammer) the large tattoo on his throat (the most painful of all to suffer, and the most likely to produce septicaemia) testified to his immediate courage; on his thighs an intricate pattern of stylized Rhinoceros hornbill heads bespoke his chiefly status; and on the top joints of his fingers a series of dots and cross-hatchings suggested that he had taken heads in battle, probably from the bodies of invading Indonesian soldiers killed in the 1962–66 confrontation by the SAS, with whom he had sometimes served as a tracker. Dignified, intelligent, full of natural authority, at forty an old man in the eyes of his tribe, he was the law-giver and judge of conduct, the arbiter of when to plant and when to harvest the padi, and, perhaps, most important of all, the chief augurer to his people, the interpreter of the messengers of the gods, the birds.

He regarded us with protective amusement. We were like the white men he had met in the war, Leon had informed us in hushed tones; we had stayed in his longhouse and behaved like guests he could trust, not offending against custom, well-mannered. James and I, in turn, decided that Tuai Rumah Dana, Lord of the House, a Beowulf, or, more accurately, a warrior-king out of Homer, was a great improvement on all our previous headmasters, deans and wardens.

Leon surfaced by the far bank of the river, half-obscured by the roots of a giant tree which twisted into the water, but obviously excited, ferociously excited. He was yelling wildly in Iban to Dana and Inghai, '*Labi-labi!*' holding his harpoon cord with both hands; and, to us, 'Fish! Round fish! Big round fish!'

Dana and Inghai leapt into the dugout and put off fast across the current. It seemed a lot of fuss about a fish, however big and round.

Dana cut two lengths of our parachute cord, one for himself and one for Inghai and, tying the boat to a branch, plunged in. Something thrashed and splashed, churning up the water between the three of them. Lowering the cord, knotted into a noose, Dana pulled it tight, secured it to the stern of the dugout; and then all three paddled back, towing something. The boat beached, they hauled on the parachute cord. Gradually, a shiny olive dome broke surface, almost round, and about three feet across. Two pairs of webbed, thick claws were thrusting against the water, front and back. Pulling it ashore in reverse, the Iban cut two holes at the rear of its carapace and threaded a lead of rattan through each slit. It 21 was a large Mud turtle, *Trionyx cartilagineus*, one of whose specific characteristics, described by a so-called closet-naturalist in the nineteenth-century British Museum from trophies in the collection, had been, as Wallace liked to point out, these very same restraining holes at the back of the shell.

Left alone for a moment, the turtle's head began to emerge from a close-fitting sleeve, from folds of telescopic muscle. It had a flexible snout for a nose, a leathery green trunk; and a sad, watery eye. Dana's *parang* came down with great violence, missing the head, glancing off the cartilaginous armour, bucking the turtle, throwing up water and pebbles. The head retracted. Dana crouched, waiting. Some ten minutes later, the turtle once more began to look cautiously for its escape. Out came the head, inch by inch. With one blow, Dana severed the neck. The head rolled, quizzically, a little way across the sand.

After a lunch of rice and sebarau, Dana and Leon heaved the turtle on to its back, slit open its white belly, and threw its guts to the fish. The meat was cut into strips, salted, and stowed away in a basket on the boat. The empty shell, the blood drying, we left on the shingle.

The river twisted and turned and grew narrower and the great creepers, tumbling down in profusion from two hundred feet above our heads, edged closer. Every now and then we would pass a tangle of river-rubbish, leaves and sticks and dead ferns, seemingly caught in the lianas by floodwater some forty feet above the present water level. So why did the high banks not show more sign of recent devastation? Idly watching one such clump as Leon arced the boat close to the bank before making a run up a rapid, we solved

the mystery. A dumpy bird, thrush-sized, its blue and yellow beak framed by whiskers, black on its back, scarlet on its stomach, popped out of a side opening: the suspended bunches of debris were the nests of the Black-and-red broadbill.

The rapids and cascades became more frequent. We had to jump out into the river more often, sometimes to our waists, sometimes to our armpits, guiding the dugout into a side channel away from the main crash of the water through the central rocks, pushing it up the shallows.

'*Saytu, dua, tiga – bata!*' sang Dana, which even we could reconstruct as one, two, three, and push.

The Iban gripped the round, algae-covered stones on the river bed easily with their muscled, calloused, spatulate toes. Our boots slipped into crevices, slithered away in the current, threatened to break off a leg at the ankle or the knee. It was only really possible to push hard when the boat was still, stuck fast, and then Headmaster Dana would shout '*Badas!*' 'Well done!' But the most welcome cry became '*Npan! Npan!*', an invitation to get back in, quick.

Crossing one such deep pool, collapsed in the boat, the engine re-started, we found ourselves staring at a gigantic Bearded pig sitting quietly on his haunches on the bank. Completely white, an old and lonely male, he looked at us with his piggy eyes. Dana, throwing his pole into the boat, snatched up his shotgun; Leon, abandoning the rudder, followed suit. Inghai shouted a warning, the canoe veered sideways into the current, the shotguns were discarded, the boat re-aligned, and the pig, no longer curious, ambled off into the jungle, his enormous testicles swaying along behind him.

We entered a wide reach of foaming water. The choppy waves, 23 snatching this way and that, had ripped caves of soil out of the banks, leaving hundreds of yards of overhang on either side. There was an ominous noise of arguing currents ahead. The rapids-preamble, the white water, the moving whirlpools, the noise ahead, was longer and louder than it ought to have been.

With the canoe pitching feverishly, we rounded a sweeping bend; and the reason for the agitated river, the unaccustomed roar, became obvious. The Green Heave ahead was very much higher than any we had met. There was a waterfall to the left of the river-course, a huge surging of water over a ledge, with the way to the right blocked by thrown-up trees, piles of roots dislodged upstream, torn out in floods, and tossed aside here against a line of rocks. There was, however, one small channel through, a shallow rapid, dangerously close to the main rush of water, but negotiable, separated from the torrent by three huge boulders.

Keeping well clear of the great whirlpool beneath the waterfall, Leon, guided between rocks by Inghai's semaphore-like gestures, brought the boat to the base of this normal-size rapid. Dana, James and I made our way carefully up with the bow-rope, while Leon and Inghai held the dugout steady.

Dana held the lead position on the rope; I stood behind him and James behind me. We pulled, Leon and Inghai pushed. The boat moved up and forward some fifteen feet and then stuck. Leon and Inghai walked up the rapid, kneeling, hunching and shoving, rolling small rocks aside to clear a channel. We waited on the lip of the rock above, pulling on the rope to keep the longboat straight, to stop it rolling sideways, tiring in the push of water round our waists. At last Leon and Inghai were ready. But the channel they had had to make was a little to our right as we looked down at them, a little to their left, a little closer to the waterfall. To pull straight we must move to our right. Dana pointed to our new positions.

It was only a stride or two. But the level of the river bed suddenly dipped, long since scooped away by the pull of the main current. James lost his footing, and, trying to save himself, let go of the rope. I stepped back and across to catch him, the rope bound round my left wrist, snatching his left hand in my right. His legs thudded into mine, tangled, and then swung free, into the current, weightless, as if a part of him had been knocked into outer space. His hat came off, hurtled past his shoes, spun in an eddy, and disappeared over the lip of the fall.

His fingers were very white; and slippery. He bites his fingernails, and they could not dig into my palm. He simply looked surprised; his head seemed a long way from me. He was feeling underwater with his free arm, impossibly trying to grip a boulder with his other hand, to get a purchase on a smooth and slimy rock, a rock polished smooth, for centuries, by perpetual tons of rolling water.

His fingers bent straighter, slowly edging out of mine, for hour upon hour, or so it felt, but it must have been in seconds. His arm rigid, his fingertips squeezed out of my fist. He turned in the current, spreadeagled. Still turning, but much faster, he was sucked under; his right ankle and shoe were bizarrely visible above the surface; he was lifted slightly, a bundle of clothes, of no discernible shape, and then he was gone.

'Boat! Boat!' shouted Dana, dropping the rope, bounding down the rocks of the side rapid, crouched, using his arms like a baboon.

'Hold the boat! Hold the boat!' yelled Leon. 25

James's bald head, white and fragile as an owl's egg, was sweeping round in the whirlpool below, spinning, bobbing up and down in the foaming water, each orbit of the current carrying him within inches of the black rocks at its edge.

Leon jumped into the boat, clambered on to the raised outboard-motor frame, squatted, and then, with a long, yodelling cry, launched himself in a great curving leap into the centre of the maelstrom. He disappeared, surfaced, shook his head, spotted James, dived again, and caught him. Inghai, too, was in the water, but, closing with them for a moment, he faltered, was overwhelmed and swept downstream. Leon, holding on to James, made a circuit of the whirlpool until, reaching the exit current, he thrust out like a turtle and they followed Inghai downriver, edging, yard by yard, towards the bank.

Obeying Dana's every sign, I helped him coax the boat on to a strip of shingle beneath the dam of logs. James, when we walked down to him, was sitting on a boulder. Leon sat beside him, an arm around his shoulders.

'You be all right soon, my friend,' said Leon. 'You be all right soon, my very best friend. Soon you be so happy.'

James, bedraggled, looking very sick, his white lips an open O in his black beard, was hyperventilating dangerously, taking great rhythmic draughts of oxygen, his body shaking.

'You be okay,' said Leon. 'I not let you die, my old friend.'

Just then little Inghai appeared, beaming with pride, holding aloft one very wet straw boater.

'I save hat!' said Inghai. 'Jams! Jams! I save hat!'

James looked up, smiled, and so stopped his terrible spasms of breathing. He really was going to be all right.

Suddenly, it all seemed funny, hilariously funny. 'Inghai saved his hat!' We laughed and laughed, rolling about on the shingle. 'Inghai saved his hat! Ingy-pingy saved his hat!' It was, I am ashamed to say, the first (and I hope it will be the last) fit of genuine medically certifiable hysterics which I have ever had.

Dana, looking at James, decided that we would camp where we were. Finding a level plateau way above the flood level on the bank behind us, the pole hut and the pole beds were soon built. I had a soap and a swim, re-covered myself in SAS super-strength insect repellent and silky crutch powder, re-filled our water bottles from the river and dosed each one with water-purifying pills, took a handful of vitamin pills myself, forced James and the Iban to take their daily measure, too, and then settled down against a boulder with my pipe (to further discourage mosquitoes), a mess-mug full of arak, and the third edition of Smythies's *The Birds of Borneo*.

James, covered in butterflies, was reading *Les Misérables* and looking a little miserable himself.

'How are you feeling?'

'Not too good, Redmond. I get these palpitations at the best of times. I've had attacks ever since Oxford. I take some special pills for it but they're really not much help. In fact the only cure is to rest a bit and then be violently sick as soon as possible.'

'Can I do anything?'

'No,' said James, pulling on his umpteenth cigarette and concentrating on Victor Hugo.

He was, I decided, an even braver old wreck than I had imagined. Looking fondly at his great bald head, I was really fairly pleased with Leon for helping the future of English literature; for preventing the disarrangement of all those brain cells; for denying all those thousands of brightly coloured little fish in the shallows the chance to nibble at torn fragments of cerebellar tissue, to ingest synapses across which had once run electrical impulses carrying stored memories of a detailed knowledge of literature in Greek and Latin, in German and French, in Spanish and Italian. But all the same, I wondered, what would we do if an accident befell us in the far interior, weeks away from any hospital, beyond the source of the Baleh, marching through the jungle towards the Tiban range and well away, even, from the stores in the boat?

Dana took his single-barrelled shotgun, held together with wire and strips of rattan, and set off to find a wild pig. Leon and Inghai went fishing with their harpoons. My Balkan Sobranie tobacco, as 90 per cent humid as everything else, tasted as rich and wet as a good gravy, and the more arak I had, the less like fermented elastoplast it became. And it actually made one see things.

A long white strip of silk chiffon detached itself from the tumultuous green tumble of trees and creepers on the opposite bank and undulated, as slowly as a lamprey in a lake, diagonally downstream. It was a very feminine apparition, redolent of everything I was beginning to miss, of silky rustles, lacy white knickers, of mysteriously intricate suspenders, of long, soft, white silk stockings dropped beside the bed. I looked at the arak with increased respect, and took some more.

A question framed itself, with great deliberation. What if, just supposing for a moment, it was not a suspender belt, but a butterfly? There were weirder things in the air in Borneo than suspender belts, after all. There was, for instance, and I planned to see it near

Mount Tiban, an owl, *Glaucidium borneense*, 'about the size of one's thumb', as Hose described it, which calls *poop-te-poop-poop*; 'and also a tiny hawk, *Microhierax*, which lays a large white egg about as big as itself'. Birds of the high montane moss forests, they 'settle on the dead trees; and as these are of a notable height, they look like insects, being in fact very much smaller than some of the large butterflies'.

In fact – perhaps it was a bird? Maybe I could identify it in Smythies without leaving my increasingly comfortable boulder to rummage for the small library in my Bergen, Home of the Ant? There it was – unmistakable, the male Paradise flycatcher, trailing two white tail feathers, each eighteen inches long. Its call is '*auk auk* very like that of a frog' (Banks), 'one of the loudest calls in the forest – both sexes call (Harrisson)'. So it was a bird that looked like a butterfly, flew like a suspender belt and sang like a frog. I fell into a deep sleep.

Leon woke me up for supper, handing me a mess-tin of sebarau and rice. Dana returned, his legs running with blood.

'What the hell's happened to him, Leon?'

'It's nothing! That's – how you say it? Leeches?'

Dana washed his legs in the river and joined us round Inghai's fire. He handed me a couple of cartridges, gesticulating angrily. The fulminite caps had been banged in by the firing pin, but the tube was still crimped, the main charge of powder unexploded. I laid them gingerly under a rock.

'They must have got wet.'

'No,' said Leon. 'Dana says Malay cartridges, Chinese cartridges, no good. English cartridges always go off, boom! He creep up on two pigs. Click. Nothing at all. He put in another. Click.

The pigs hear him. Foof. They run away. So no *babi*. No roast *babi* in a pot. Only fishes stew.'

'Leon,' I said, 'why did you cry like that, when you saved James's life?'

'Well,' said Leon, shuffling his bare feet on the sand, 'we Christians like you, of course, but, all the same, we respect the river. The river like Jams. The river take Jams away. So we say sorries to the river, because we take him back again.'

James was picking at his bony fish in the mess-tin, pushing his rice aside.

'Excuse me,' he said, got up, lurched a little, and was horribly sick into a bush.

'Now, you better, my best friend,' said Leon. 'Now I give you more rices. *Makai!* Eat up! *Makai*, Jams!'

The sky grew black suddenly. There was an odd breeze. Everyone – insects, monkeys, birds, frogs – stopped making a noise. Dana, Leon and Inghai ran to the dugout, dragged it high up the shingle and re-tied it, bow and stern, with long ropes leading to trees on the high bank. Huge globules of water began to fall, splashing star-burst patterns on the dry hot rocks along the shore. We made for the *bashas*, changed fast, and slipped inside. Rain splattered on the tree canopy two hundred feet above, a whispery noise growing duller and increasing in volume to a low drumming. Drops hit our canvas awnings and bounced off; a fine spray came sideways through the mosquito net. A wind arrived; and we heard the first tree start its long crashing fall far off in the forest. Thunder rumbled nearer, and, every few seconds, the trunks of the trees immediately in view through the triangular gap at the foot of the *basha* were bright with lightning flashes, reflected power from balls and sheets and zig-zags of light, energy that lit the clumps of lichen on the bark with startling clarity, that picked out the tendrils of fungus and the stalks of spore-bodies like heads of unkempt hair.

I fell asleep and I dreamed of James's sister Chotty. She was coming at me with a particular knife she uses to make her beef stews, her pheasant pies. 'It's quite all right,' she said. 'It doesn't matter now that he's drowned. There's no need to apologize. I don't want to hear your explanations.'

In the morning, the world was soaked, the mist was thick, and the river had risen five or six feet. After a breakfast of rice and fish, James and I walked ahead up the steeply sloping bank and Dana and Leon and Inghai easily brought the boat up the now deeper side rapid. The water was full of broken branches, old logs which had broken free from their previous snags, ferns, lengths of creeper and mud. A dead green bird like a parakeet, perhaps a Green broadbill, floated past.

Dana confined James to the boat, or else put us ashore beneath a rapid, making us walk up and round it and picking us up beside the pools above; but in any case the temporary change in water level made the going easier, submerging some cataracts altogether, filling channels through others. We had almost grown accustomed to the kingfishers, the herons, the fish-eagles that escorted us ahead. But there was one bird that always puzzled me, a new concept in eagles, occasionally wheeling over us, screaming its shrill cry, repeating it again and again. Sometimes it made this call and it was black; sometimes it made the same call and it was white, and brown-barred under the wings. One of them might have been Blyth's Hawk eagle, but for the cry. Probably, as Smythies told us, it was the Changeable hawk eagle, an odd species in which, in part-defiance of Darwin's rules for the mechanism of sexual selection, the two different plumages are haphazardly distributed with no apparent regard for male or female, age or range.

We made good progress, twisting and turning and rising up the narrowing river for mile upon mile. At one point, where the river split into two around an island, the trees on either bank were so close together that their branches touched and, over our heads, a troop of Pig-tailed macaques, on all fours, their tails slightly curled and held up in the air behind them, like those of so many cats pleased to be home, were making an aerial crossing. They scrutinized us for a moment or two, and then scampered for cover.

Further up, in a massively buttressed oak-like tree, sat something large and furry, a rich, mahogany red back and side of fur with its head obscured by leaves. Just for a moment, I thought it might be an orang-utan, but had to admit that it was scarcely probable; we were far more likely to have caught a glimpse of a Maroon leaf monkey, Hose's Maroon langur.

In any case, it was just then that James promised to see something marvellous, having, I believe, seen it already. High up, circling in a sky which at that time of day can look almost English, heat-wave, August-blue with a fluff of clouds, were two enormous eagles, pitch-black, their tails surprisingly long: Black eagles.

The river became shallower as the day wore on and once again I had to push the boat, almost continuously. It was shattering work, heaving against the current, falling over the stones on the river bed. The Iban were as fit as men could be, but an extra source of energy fuelled them, too; could it simply be the rice they ate, at each meal, some twelve times more than us, some twelve times more than one would have thought possible? I resolved to mimic Leon's diet in every particular.

At lunchtime, Leon harpooned a river tortoise, about eighteen inches long with a muddy black carapace and its plastron flat and blotched with yellow and black. He was stowed, sadly, beneath the duckboards of the dugout. Inghai caught yet more sebarau, and we roasted them over an open fire. Expecting to keel over like a blown bull at any moment, to explode disgustingly among the rocks, I forced myself to eat as much sticky, finger-gluing rice as Leon did, to the great approval of the Iban and the horror of the Fenton Life began to seem even better, and much rounder.

Putting up the *bashas* that evening, I heard a rushing noise above the trees, like the wings of swans.

'Hornbills! Hornbills!'

'*Tajai! Tajai!*' shouted Dana, running for his gun.

'No, no, Leon. Tell him not to shoot!'

The two great birds, larger than swans, four feet across the wings, flew heavily over the river, unperturbed by our shouting. Their long tail plumes trailing, their wings making a whooshing noise with each stroke, they alternately flapped and sailed, labouring and gliding into the topmost branches of a dead tree on the far bank. Bespattered with white droppings, it was obviously a favourite perch. I watched them through the binoculars, through the small clear patch of lens which had not yet succumbed to the all-encroaching fungus growing within the tubes.

Their necks were feathery orange; the solid ivory casques, the square block-mountings on top of their bills, were red and yellow. Ruffling their feathers, they looked at us, and flapped away from view into the canopy of tree tops. But, in a moment or two, they began their extraordinary calling, a series of strong hoots getting louder and quicker and more excited and ending in a burst of dirty hilarity, *cack-cack-cack-cackle*. Other birds joined in. And then we heard a different sound, a loud succession of barking, roaring calls.

'*Kenyalang!*' said Dana, beaming. '*Badas!*'

'It's good lucks,' said Leon. 'It's our *gawai* bird. Very important bird for we Iban.'

Dana called, a deep raven call, and the bird answered.

'We have very good lucks, and now we cook the turtle,' said Leon.

The hornbills kept calling, allowing me to check their notes against their score in Smythies. *Kenyalang* was the Rhinoceros hornbill, a bird central to Iban ritual, and *Tajai* was indeed the Helmeted hornbill, whose ivory was once more valuable than jade, and was traded from Borneo to China certainly at the time of the first Ming Emperor, and probably long before. As for the Rhinoceros hornbill ceremonies, I resolved to screw the anthropological secrets, if there were any, out of Leon later.

Hunks of turtle meat were a great improvement on weak sebarau flesh and strong sebarau needle-bones, but the tightly compacted, powerful muscles were tough to eat. It was a Wrigley's Mudmint Chewing Gum Turtle. Still masticating my strip of *Trionyx sub-plaňus* two hours later, I went to bed to read about hornbills. Hose, I decided, in *The Field-book of a Jungle-wallah*, had the best
34 description of their nesting habits.

All the species build their home, for protection, in a hollow tree, communication with the outer world being by means of a slit or hole. If this opening is not at the right elevation above the floor of the nest the birds fill up the interior with leaves and twigs until it is the right height for the mother-bird to be able to sit comfortably on her eggs with her beak protruding so as to receive food. This having been arranged satisfactorily, the hen bird spreads a thin layer of feathers plucked from her own body on the built-up floor, and is then completely walled up by the male, who plasters over the opening with a sort of gummy substance which he secretes in his stomach; this substance hardens on exposure to the air and shuts in the female until her beak alone shows. In this uncomfortable position she remains a prisoner until her nestlings are from two to three weeks old, the male feeding her meanwhile with insects, fruit, seeds, and parts of frogs and lizards, all rolled up into a sort of pellet, which he throws into the expectant beak of his mate.

When feeding the female, the cock bird clings to the bark of the tree, or else perches on a convenient branch, and jerks the food into his wife's beak. I knew one instance where, the husband-bird having been shot by hunters, other males came and supported the widow. While the feeding and imprisonment process is going on, several seeds naturally are not caught by the hen, and falling to the ground germinate; by observing the growth of these, the natives can infer the age of the young birds without seeing them.

The native method of catching the mother-bird during the period of incubation is rather brutal. The tree is scaled and the entrance broken open; the frightened bird flutters up the hollow trunk but is brought down with a thorny stick which is thrust in after her and twisted about until a firm grip is obtained of both her flesh and plumage.

Hornbills make amusing and interesting pets, for they become quite tame and will follow their owner about like a dog. One that I had at Claudetown became quite an expert at catching bananas thrown him. On one occasion the late Rajah was staying with me and was surprised over his morning tea and fruit by my pet, who coolly perched on the railing of the verandah. Taken aback by the grotesque creature, he looked round for something to throw at it, but while his head was turned for a second, a whirring noise was heard and his breakfast was gone.

I fell asleep, and nightmares returned. I lay stuck fast, fat with Inghai's greasy rice, white with SAS anti-fungus skin powder, at the dark base of a hornbill hole in some Freudian tree. There was a cracking noise above my head and the entrance burst apart. With great difficulty, the wreaths of flesh round my neck squashing against the bark, I looked up. Chotty was enlarging the opening with a meat hammer. She looked in, a thorny stick in her other hand. 'Of course, it doesn't matter now he's drowned,' she said, 'but you should have placed yourself *behind* him on the rope.'

The next day the river became more difficult still: an unending series of rapids and snags and boulders. The dugout seemed to increase its weight with every mile; the 120°F heat, bearing down and beating off the surface of the water seemed less easy to struggle through, even when the warm water was up to one's neck. Two towels bound round my head failed to keep the sweat out of my eyes and off my glasses.

There were fewer laughs at lunchtime on the shingle. The river was too low, said Dana, the going too tough. We now needed two small canoes instead of one big one. Only Leon, immensely strong, cheerful and affectionate, was undaunted. He was obviously a champion river-hunter, too: while we lay, exhausted, in the shade of a jungle chestnut tree, he disappeared, swimming underwater up an adjacent creek. Half an hour later he returned, towing a fresh trophy. It was much longer than he was: a big Water monitor, a black and yellow prehistoric dragon with a long forked tongue which it protruded like a snake. Dana and Leon pulled it up the bank. It stood four-square, clear of the ground, hissing, and lashing its long tail, the harpoon stuck through its side. Dana drew his *parang* and killed it with a blow to the head.

The lizard strapped into the dugout, we set off again. It was too arduous to notice much – for hour upon hour I was only really conscious of the whirling water, the side of the boat and my own gripping positions on the gunwale. But then the country began to open out, the big trees stepped back from the bank; rolling hills, covered with nothing but young scrub jungle, stretched away to a forest horizon. The Iban looked about them uneasily. There was no mark of all this on our secret government maps.

We continued on our way for a mile or so and then, glancing up, I found myself looking into the big brown eyes of a girl on the bank beside us. She was standing in a loose clump of bamboo, her fine black hair falling over her bare shoulders and breasts.

'Kayan?' shouted Dana.

The girl turned and fled.

A little further on, four men, in two small canoes, were setting nets.

'Kayan?' Dana repeated.

'Kenyah!' shouted the men, much insulted. They yelled instructions above the noise of the water, pointing upriver.

'Can you understand them, Leon?'

'No,' said Leon, uncharacteristically quiet. 'These are not our peoples.'

The river meandered, grew broader and more shallow, and then   37 entered a very long straight reach. A paradise was disclosed. An inland kingdom, secluded almost beyond reach, of padi fields and banana trees, palms and coconuts, lay in its own wide valley, surrounded by jungle hills; a huge longhouse, its *atap* roof blending into the landscape, was set back from the left bank of the river, about three miles off; some forest giants had been left standing, here and there, and on one of these a pair of Brahminy kites were sitting, the birds of Singalang Burong, King of the Gods.

Cheered by amused men in light fishing canoes and by families from their farms on the banks, it took us two hours to manhandle the heavy dugout up to the beach beneath the longhouse.

About to wade ashore, Dana stopped me emphatically, pointing me to my place on the duckboards.

'We must waits,' said Leon. 'This not our country.'

About sixty children watched us silently from the bank. Some of their mothers, their ear lobes, weighted by brass rings, dangling down below their shoulders, watched too. In about a quarter of an hour, after much to-ing and fro-ing, the chief's son arrived and formally invited us to set foot on his tribal lands.

Heaving the Bergens on to our backs, we followed him towards the longhouse along a network of paths laid out between the padi stores, huts on stilts, each with its own ladder and with a close-fitting down-turned plate of wood set around each stilt to keep out the rats. The settlement was obviously large and well organized. Even the dogs looked young and healthy. And the longhouse, when we reached it, was spectacular. Massively constructed on tree-trunk piles and a forest of lesser stilts, it was about three hundred yards long, the main floor set fifteen feet from the ground. Dark, hairy, boar-like pigs, indistinguishable from the Wild bearded pigs of the jungle, rooted and grunted among the garbage between the poles; chickens, the cockerels looking as magnificent as the ancestral Jungle fowl, scratched about among the pigs, and favourite dogs, stretched out on the side of the verandah, lolled their heads over the edge of the bamboo platform and observed our arrival with mild interest.

Climbing a slippery notched log up to a longhouse with a sixty-pound Bergen on one's back is not easy, and I went up the muddy trunk almost on all fours, holding on hard with both hands. The Iban and the chief's son paused while James and I took our shoes off; we then crossed the outer apron and the roofed verandah and were ushered into the chief's quarters. The room stretched, at right angles, back from the line of the longhouse for about a hundred feet. It was cross-beamed and triangularly roofed like a barn, the huge timbers cross-cut into one another and lashed with rattan. There were several sleeping platforms, some with curtains, some with bamboo partitions round them, down one side of the room. The chief's son, smaller, fairer-skinned than the Iban, but just as muscular and just as dignified, indicated a patch of floor where we might sleep. Dana and he, to their mutual delight, began to talk, albeit with no great fluency.

'They very clever mens,' said Leon, 'they both talk Kayan.'

'Can you talk Kayan?'

Leon grinned.

'Only very dirty words. A girl she told them to me. A very silly Kayan girls. But I talk English.'

'Well, you'll have to translate *everything*. You'll have to help us – you ask Dana what they're saying.'

Leon and Dana talked rapidly in Iban.

'The son of the chief says he very sorries. Almost all the people are in the fields, but they come back tonight. The chief is away on the Mahakam.'

'The Mahakam?'

'These people they come from there. They come fifteen years ago. This good land, very good.'

So they had crossed over the mountains from the great Mahakam basin, from Indonesia, from the river that flowed south-east into the Makassir Strait.

'We have fun tonight,' said Leon.

I awoke instantly from a passing reverie, a realization that we must be within striking distance of the centre of Borneo, perhaps almost within reach of the wild, nomadic, primitive peoples, the Ukit, the men who could tell us, if anyone could, whether or no the Borneo rhinoceros was still to be found.

'Hey, Leon,' I said, a little too anxiously, 'step outside a minute, will you? I've something very important to tell you.'

'Eh?'

'Come on.'

Out on the verandah, I grabbed his tattooed arm. 'Look – don't tell James, because he wouldn't like it, he's so modest. But, in England, he's *very* famous. He is the poet of all the tribe, the chief poet in all England. His *whole life* is making songs. That's what he does all day. You understand? He *sings songs*. And he dances. He knows *all* the dances.'

Leon was genuinely excited, immensely impressed.

'So look, Leon, between now and tonight, tell everyone – or else James will just sit there – you tell everyone, via Dana, that James is the greatest poet in all England and that when it's our turn to dance and sing, they must shout for James. Okay? Will you do that?'

'He very great man,' said Leon. 'Very old. Very serious man. I tell Dana.'

We began to unpack; and a crowd started to gather. The oldest woman I had yet seen in Borneo, squatting on the floor, her wrinkled breasts and her ear lobes hanging forlornly, her attitude one of exaggerated distress, was alternately touching my leg and theatrically placing her hands over her eyes. I assumed that, sensibly enough, she found the sight of me painful beyond endurance and wanted this white tramp out of her drawing-room, fast. After all, with a half-grown beard, river-and-sweat-soaked shirt, water-frayed trousers and socks, and already inescapably possessed of the sweet, fetid, rotting smell of the jungle, I was even less of a truffle for the senses than usual. But I suddenly realized that she was asking for help. Her old eyes were bloodshot, her eyelids swollen. Feeling useful and needed, I pulled out my medicine pack and found the antibiotic eye drops. Smiling broadly she disclosed her gums. Not a tooth to be seen. I squeezed in some drops and she clapped her hands.

A mother pressed forward, holding up her baby's arm. There was an angry red mound of infection on it, just below the shoulder joint. Perhaps this was the ringworm that Harrisson wrote about.

'*Kurap?*' I asked.

She nodded, impatiently. I put Savlon and a dressing on the wound, covering up the skin which was split like a rotten tomato, and weeping like one. A queue of mothers and children formed; we dressed hundreds of cuts that had gone septic, small ulcers, patches of skin fungus, rashes. And then the men began to trickle 41 in. They mimed, with a suppleness, a balletic grace that would have impressed Nijinsky, excruciating, disabling back pain; with eyes as big and bright as those of a fox hunting in the dusk they indicated that they were suffering from the kind of headaches that amount to concussion; with contortions that would have torn Houdini into spare ribs they demonstrated that their stomachs had ceased to function, that they were debilitated almost beyond assistance.

'Multivite,' I announced, with great solemnity.

'Alka-seltzer,' said James, as one who practised it.

I put two bright orange pills in each extended palm. Some swallowed. Some chewed. Everyone looked happy.

The eight tablets, as white and round and efficacious as sacred slices of pig tusk, sat in the bottom of James's mess-tin. Gurgle, gurgle went his upturned water bottle, and the roundels spun and bubbled and talked to each other and grew as thin as excised circles of feather cut from the very tip of the tail of the hornbill. Throwing up spray, foaming like the river in a rapid, the water rose up in the tin. The Kenyah crowded round tight, and looked in.

'Drink,' said James, handing it to the first man and staring at him like a shaman. The patient shut his eyes, mumbled something, and took a mouthful. 'Aaah!' he gasped, passing it on, wiping the fizz from his lips. 'Aah!' said everyone in turn, straightening out at once, squaring their powerful shoulders. There would be no backache tonight.

Trying to resume our unpacking and, most pressing of all, to change into our dry clothes, I dislodged the sealed bag of picture postcards of the Queen on horseback, Trooping the Colour. An idea presented itself: the Sovereign would save me from undue scrutiny in the transition between pairs of trousers.

'Look,' I said, 'this is for you. Here is our Tuai Rumah, our chief in England.'

'Inglang!' said the children. The cards were sheeny and metallic, the kind that change the position of their subjects as their own position is changed against the light.

I gave one to a little boy. He looked at it with amazed delight: he turned it this way and that; he scratched it and waited to see what would happen; he whipped it over, to catch a glimpse of Her Majesty from the back. Small hands thrust up like a clump of bamboo; the old woman, annoyed, demanded a pile for herself. If the children had one each, the men wanted more than one each. In five minutes, four hundred mementoes of the Empire disappeared.

There were now so many people in the room that I really wanted a photograph: with, I imagined, great stealth, I held a Fuji to my stomach, pointed it in the right direction, looked the other way myself, and pressed the button. Chaos ensued. Children howled, the women pulled their sarongs over their breasts, the men looked annoyed.

'Quick, quick – get the Polaroid,' hissed James.

With an elaborate enactment of deep apology, followed by circus gestures promising fun to come, great tricks, something quite different, and not at all offensive, I drew out the Polaroid and loaded it. The grey box would take away their image, I tried to suggest with both hands, and then give it back again. They looked dubious. I had behaved badly once, and was not really to be trusted.

The Polaroid flashed; we waited; the box whirred; the tray slid forward and proffered its wet card. I laid it on the floor, waving their fingers away. Slowly, it grew colours, like bacteria in a dish of culture. The room was very silent. They watched the outlines of heads and shoulders appear; features became defined. Suddenly they pointed to the card and to each other. Wild hilarity erupted. They clapped and clapped. They ran off to change into their best clothes and we, at last, put on our dry trousers. Only the old woman was left to grimace in astonishment, or disgust, at the whiteness, or the hairiness, of our legs.

Proudly wearing garish sarongs or Chinese shorts and T-shirts which had been traded downriver in the rainy season, presumably, for turtles or deer or pig, for camphor or gutta-percha or rattan or pepper, they arranged themselves into family groups, forcing me to shuttle their images in and their pictures out, until the Polaroid grew hot and all the film was finished.

'What a lot of children everyone has,' I observed to Leon.

'No, no,' said Leon, 'the mothers and the fathers – they die. My own parents, they die too, sickness, or cutting trees, *shick-shick*,' said Leon, miming the curving descent of a *parang* blade, 'or in the river, bang heads on the rocks, or poison-fish, or in the jungle, hunting. You have cut. You have boil. Very painful. You have very good lucks to get better. Then you must be adopted. I adopted. My uncle and my aunt. Very kind peoples. Or the peoples in the *bileks* [rooms] next door. They must take the children.'

So these magnificent warrior-farmers, I thought, looking round at so much health and so much glowing muscle, at so many beautiful faces and breasts and smiles and jangling earrings, are the product of evolution by natural selection almost in its crudest sense.

The chief's son ushered everyone out of the huge room. We must be hungry, he said (we were); his mother and his sisters had cooked the monitor lizard (perhaps we were not quite that hungry). At the far end of the room there was a fire of split logs with a massive piece of ironwood for a hearth. A series of pots were suspended above it, and the smoke made its way out through a propped-open flap in the roof.

The girls left our mess-tins and plates in a circle round a piled bowl of rice and the hindquarters of the monitor lizard, and then withdrew. Dana served me a helping of tail, the last ten inches of it, or thereabouts; and the resin lamps flickered, and the sows and boars and piglets grunted and squealed on the rubbish and pig shit below the floorboards; and the geckos chick-chacked to each other in the roof spaces like mating sparrows; and I realized that the yellow-and-black-skinned monitor-lizard tail would not disappear from my tin, as custom demanded, until I ate it myself.

'*Makai! Makai!*' said Dana.

The flesh was yellow and softish and smelt bad, very like the stray chunks of solid matter in the effluvia one sees in England on an unwashed pavement outside a public house late on a Saturday night. I eased it off the small vertebrae, mixed it into the sticky rice, and told myself that even this particular meal would all be over one day.

The Iban ate fast and went out for a swim in the river and a wash. We finished our supper, more or less, but felt momentarily far too sick to swim in the dark. The girls cleared everything away. Returning, looking very clean, Dana, Leon and Inghai put on their most dazzling trousers and T-shirts. They then, with great deliberation, took turns with Dana's piece of broken mirror and his rusty tweezers to pluck out any hairs that might have sprouted unbeknown upon their chins or cheeks. Leon sported a straggly thin

45

moustache which he later shaved away, but in general the races of Borneo are almost hairless, and they dislike any growth on the face intensely. They certainly disliked ours. It amused me to think that Darwin himself had run into logical trouble attempting to argue away this awkward anomaly in his scheme for the differential advancement of races.

Some races are much more hairy than others [he writes in *The Descent of Man*], especially the males; but it must not be assumed that the more hairy races, such as the European, have retained their primordial condition more completely than the naked races, such as the Kalmucks or Americans. It is more probable that the hairiness of the former is due to partial reversion; for characters which have been at some former period long inherited, are always apt to return. We have seen that idiots are often very hairy, and they are able to revert in other characters to a lower animal type.

Suddenly, a wave of sound made its way into the room from the long gallery outside, simple melodies beautifully sung, a clear chorus of young voices which swept over us and out through the thin bamboo walls to the padi fields and the jungle beyond. Surprised, we went to investigate. The youth of the longhouse was assembled in rows, singing hymns in Kenyah.

'Roman Catholics,' said Leon. 'Very good. But we have fun later.'

'Who converted them?'

'The missionaries, of course. The other side. They bring it with them.'

It was an odd idea indeed, Roman Catholic missionaries in ex-Dutch Borneo, at the very headwaters of the Mahakam. A middle-aged man beat time with a stick, a battered green hymn book in his other hand. The singing went on and on; but eventually the meeting was over, and the flaming youth of Nanga Sinyut dispersed.

We were very tired. It was all too confusing; the river seemed to have spun cat's-cradles of pain out of all the muscle fibres in my calves and back; and the monitor lizard's tail was still gently whisking, from side to side, in my stomach. I took a long pull at the arak can and lay down on the floor of the chief's room. The huge cross-beams of the roof bucked and twisted and stuck fast on some celestial river floating over my head: I fell asleep.

'Come on,' shouted James, from a bank far away to my right, 'get up! There's going to be a welcome party.'

Staggering out, wanting to sleep as never before, I looked around, and wished I was somewhere else. The gallery was packed. The lamps had been lit. *Tuak* was being drunk. A long, uninviting space had been cleared in front of part of the line of longhouse doors; and around its three sides sat an expectant audience.

Leon and Inghai, looking fresh and eager, beckoned us to the back row. Dana was nowhere to be seen. He was, as Leon explained, as befitted his high and kingly status, drinking with the deputy chief of all the Kenyah on the Baleh, and was not to be disturbed, because, being Absolute Chief of all the Iban of Kapit District, he had many cares, and would soon be taking a sleeps.

We were given a glass of *tuak*. A tray of huge, cone-shaped cheroots of Kenyah tobacco wrapped in leaves and each tied with a bow of leaf-strips was passed round; a sinuous young girl put ours in our mouths and lit them with a taper. I noticed that Leon was wearing his large and flashy, supposedly waterproof, digital watch. After its first celebratory dive with Leon into the depths of the Rajang this watch had ceased to tell the time, but it would still, if shaken violently enough, and to Leon's unvarying delight, sound its alarm.

The musicians sat in front of us. An old man held a *keluri*, a dried gourd shaped like a chemical retort but held upwards, and with six bamboo pipes projecting in a bundle from its bulb; a group of young men sat ready with a bamboo harp (a tube of bamboo with raised strips cut from its surface), a bamboo xylophone, a bamboo flute, and a single-stringed instrument, a dugout-canoe-like sounding box carved from a single block of wood, the string so heavy it had to be pulled with an iron hook.

The chief's son entered, transformed. On his head he wore a war helmet, a woven rattan cap set with black and yellow and crimson beads, topped with six long black and white plumes from the tail of the Helmeted hornbill. He was dressed in a war coat, made from the skin of the largest cat in Borneo, the Clouded leopard. His head placed through an opening at the front of the skin, the bulk stretched down his back, and on to it were fastened row upon row of Rhinoceros hornbill feathers. Around his waist, slung on a silver belt and sheathed in a silver scabbard, was a *parang* to outshine all other *parangs*, its hilt intricately carved in horn from the antler of the *kijang*, the big Borneo deer. In his left hand, his arm crooked behind it, he carried a long shield, pointed at both ends, and from the centre of which a huge mask regarded us implacably, its eyes red, its teeth the painted tusks of the wild boar. Thick black tufts of hair hung in neat lines down either edge and across the top and bottom, tufts of hair which, we were led to believe, had long ago been taken from the scalps of heads cut off in battle.

Laying the ancient, and presumably fragile, shield carefully against the wall, the warrior took up his position at the centre of the floor. He crouched down and, at a nod from the man on the base string, a hollow, complicated, urgent, rhythmic music began. With exaggerated movements, his thigh muscles bunching and loosening, his tendons taut, a fierce concentration on his face, the chief's son turned slowly in time with the music, first on one foot and then on the other, rising, inch by inch, to his own height, apparently peering over some imaginary cover. Sighting the enemy, he crouched again, and then, as the music quickened, he drew his bright *parang* and leapt violently forward, weaving and dodging, with immense exertion, cutting and striking, parrying unseen blows with his mimed shield. For a small second, his ghostly foe was off-guard, tripped on the shingle, and the heir to the Lordship of all the Kenyah of Nanga Sinyut claimed his victory with one malicious blow.

Everyone clapped and cheered, and so did I. Five young girls rushed forward to take off the hero's hornbill helmet, and war coat, and *parang*. It was wonderful. The girls were very beautiful. All was right with the world. And then I realized, as a Rajah Brooke's birdwing took a flap around my duodenum, that the beautiful girls, in a troop, were coming, watched by all the longhouse, for me.

'You'll be all right,' said James, full of *tuak*. 'Just do your thing. Whatever it is.'

Strapped into the war coat and the *parang*, the hornbill feathers on my head, I had a good idea. It would be a simple procedure to copy the basic steps that the chief's son had just shown us. There really was not much to it, after all. The music struck up, sounding just a little bit stranger than it had before.

I began the slow crouch on one leg, turning slightly. Perhaps, actually, this was a mistake, I decided. Ghastly pains ran up my thighs. Terminal cramp hit both buttocks at once. Some silly girl began to titter. A paraplegic wobble spread down my back. The silly girl began to laugh. Very slowly, the floor came up to say hello, and I lay down on it. There was uproar in the longhouse. How very funny, indeed.

Standing up, I reasoned that phase two would be easier. Peering over the imaginary boulder, I found myself looking straight into the eyes of an old man on the far side of the verandah. The old fool was crying with laughter, his ridiculous long ears waggling about. Drawing the *parang*, which was so badly aligned that it stuck in the belt and nearly took my fingers off, I advanced upon the foe, jumping this way and that, feeling dangerous. The old man fell off his seat. There was so much misplaced mirth, so much plain howling, that I could not hear the music, and so perhaps my rhythm was not quite right.

'Redsi!' came an unmistakable shout. 'Why don't you improvise?'

Stabbed in the back just as I was about to take my very first head, I spun round violently to glare at the Fenton. I never actually saw him, because the cord of the war helmet, not used to such movements, slipped up over the back of my head, and the helmet itself, flying forward, jammed fast over my face. Involuntarily, I took a deep gasp of its sweat-smooth rattan interior, of the hair of generations of Kenyah warriors who had each been desperate to impress the girls of their choice. It was an old and acrid smell.

The boards were shaking. The audience was out of control. And then, just in time, before suffocation set in, the five girls, grossly amused, set me free.

'Go and get James,' I spluttered. 'You go and get James.'

'Now you sing song,' shouted Leon.

'No, no – James sing songs.'

'Jams!' shouted Leon, remembering his mission.

'Jams!' The longhouse reverberated. 'Jams! Jams!' Leon had done his work well.

With great theatrical presence, offering almost no resistance to the five young girls, James processed on to the stage. The Kenyah fell silent. T. D. Freeman, in his work on Iban augury, tells us that the King of the Gods, Singalang Burong, may well be encountered in dreams. There is no mistaking him. He is almost as old as the trees, awe-inspiring, massive of body, and, a characteristic which puts his identity beyond doubt, completely bald. Judging by the slightly uneasy, deferential, expectant faces around me, Bali Penyalong, the High God of the Kenyah, was but a different name for the same deity.

The attendants withdrew. James, resplendent in leopard skin and hornbill feathers, looked even more solemn than is his habit. With the accumulated experience of many thousands of evenings at the theatre, of years of drama criticism, he regarded his audience; his huge brown eyes appeared to fix on everyone in turn. There was some backward shuffling in the front row. A dog whimpered.

The music began, a little shakily. James, in time with the music, began to mime. He was hunting something, in a perfunctory way; he made rootling movements with his head, and grunted. He was hunting a pig. Evidently successful, he butchered his quarry, selected the joint he had in mind, hung the carcase from a hook in the

51

roof and betook himself to his ideal kitchen. Passion entered the show; James began to concentrate; his gestures quickened and the mesmerized musicians increased their tempo. He scored the pork; he basted it; he tied it with string; he made extraordinarily complex sauces; he cooked potatoes and sprouts and peas and beans and broccoli and *zucchini*, I think, until they were *fritti*. After many a tasting and many an alchemical manoeuvre with a *batterie de cuisine* decidedly better than Magny's, James deemed the gravy to be perfect. The apple sauce was plentiful. The decanted Burgundy was poured into a glass. James looked fondly at his creation and began to eat. The crackling crackled between his teeth. The warriors of the Kenyah, as if they had been present at a feast of the Gods, rose to their feet and burped. Everybody cheered.

'Jams very hungry,' said Leon to me confidentially. 'He must eat more rices.'

James held up a hand. Everyone sat down again, cross-legged. 'And now,' he announced, 'we will have a sing-song.'

'Inglang song! Inglang song!' shouted Inghai, wildly excited, and full of *arak*.

And then James really did astonish me. To the beat of the big string he launched into a rhyming ballad, a long spontaneous poem about our coming from a far country, entering the Rajang from the sea, about the pleasures of the Baleh and the danger of the rapids and the hospitality of the strongest, the most beautiful people in all the world, the Kenyah of Nanga Sinyut.

I clapped as wildly as Inghai. 'Bravo, Jams!' I shouted; 'Bravo, Jams!' mimicked Inghai; 'Bravo! Bravo!' sang the Kenyah.

James indicated that he was tired; he pillowed his black-and-white-plumed head on his hands. But it was no use. We wanted more songs. We wanted so many, in fact, that I discovered, to my amazement, that he knew almost every popular and music-hall song back to about 1910 and that he could adapt their tunes to the vagaries of the bamboo gourd-pipes with professional ease.

James was saved, just before he collapsed from exhaustion, when the longhouse clown stood up, jealous of his great success. The helmet and coat were laid aside, and James sat down. But my annoyance was short-lived. People began to laugh before the clown had done anything at all, and it soon became obvious that he was a very witty Fool indeed.

With exaggerated seriousness, he sat on the floor, his legs out-stretched; he put on an imaginary hat and he fastened his imaginary shirtcuffs. He looked about, unconcerned, like a great chief.

'It's Jams!' said Leon. 'It's Jams in the boat! He very serious man!'

'Jams!' said the Kenyah, laughing with recognition and approval.

The clown then got out of the longboat and became a Neander-thaler, struggling in the river, pulling the dugout this way and that, always getting it wrong, unable to walk and push at the same time, his movements constantly directed, with a frantic exasper-ation of contradictory gestures, by Dana and Leon and Inghai. There were roars of laughter.

'It's Redmon!' said Leon. 'He very fats!'

The chief's son then stood up and announced something. The long gallery became quiet again. He pointed to about fifteen men, in turn, who followed him on to the floor. They were all young and eager, bodily alert, absurdly fit. Long-backed, with fairly short, lavishly muscled limbs, they looked like athletes at the peak of their careers, assembling at the Olympics for the men's pentathlon.

'They all bachelors,' whispered Leon. 'They not yet picked their womens.'

The men formed into a single line, by order of height. And a completely different kind of music began, violent, aggressive, with a menacing and insistent beat. They walked slowly forward, unsmiling, stamping their feet, looking rhythmically to either side, intent. This, I realized, was the dance described in Hose, albeit the protagonists were wearing shorts and singlets:

The bigger boys are taught to take part in the dance in which the return from the warpath is dramatically represented. This is a musical march rather than a dance. A party of young men in full war dress form up in single line; the leader, and perhaps two or three others, play the battle march on the *keluri*. The line advances slowly up the gallery, each man turning half about at every third step, the even numbers turning to the one hand, the odd to the other hand, alternately, and all stamping together as they complete the turn at each third step. The turning to right and left symbolizes the alert guarding of the heads which are supposed to be carried by the victorious warriors.

After five march-pasts, as I was deciding that this would not be a sensible longhouse to attack even if one really was in the SAS, everyone relaxed, and we were invited to join the line. James picked up the rhythm at once, but I found even these steps difficult, falling over my boots. All the girls giggled.

'Redmon,' said Leon, when we sat down again, 'you so big, your feet too far from your head.'

'That's it. That's exactly what it is.'

There was a pause.

'Or, maybe,' said Leon, 'you so fats you can't see them.'

Leon, with gross bad manners, uncrossed his legs, lay flat out on the floor, and laughed at his own joke, redirecting his attention, sharply, only when the unmarried girls stood up.

Gracefully, shyly, the young girls aligned themselves.

'Look at that one,' said Leon, 'look at that one in the pink sarong. Redmon. Just *look* at that one.'

'Behave yourself,' I said, testily. 'This is no time for one of your jumps. You'll get us all killed.'

'She the moon in the sky,' said Leon.

The girls, to a delicate, lilting dance tune, began their own movement across the long stage and back again; lithe, slender, very young, they were indeed lovely to look at; and their dance was deliciously fragile after the violence of the men. With small, flowing movements of their wrists and fingers, all in synchrony, their arms rippling, their supple bodies undulating slightly, they mimicked the leisurely flight of the hornbill. The forward step on the beat outlined the legs beneath their folded-down sarongs. The gentle, backward swaying, on the pause, revealed the tight breasts beneath their T-shirts.

Leon's eyes were wide, as wide as they had been when he shot his turtle. I blew in his ear.

'Shush,' said Leon. 'You be quiets. Now we watch.'

Looking round to poke Inghai, I saw that he was asleep, curled up on the floor, still holding his *arak* mug in both hands. All the men were very quiet.

Far too soon, the dance was over. We clapped, adoringly, sentimentally, soppily, feeling a little weak. The girls, blushing, scurried to their seats and giggled. But the girl in the pink sarong returned, carrying two huge bunches of hornbill feathers. They were strapped to her wrists, set out and fixed like an open fan. Her

55

features were strikingly beautiful, certainly; her hair, about a foot longer than that of the other girls, was combed down, loose and fine, black and silky, to her waist. Her looped ear lobes, weighted with rings, hung down only to the base of her smooth neck, soft and brown in the light of the lamp. The tattoos on her arms were only half-complete and, as tattooing begins in a girl's tenth year and continues in small bouts at regular intervals (otherwise the pain of the operation would be insupportable and the ensuing inflammation probably fatal), she could be, I calculated, no more than fourteen or fifteen years old.

'Leon,' I said, 'she's far too young. She's only fourteen.'

'What is it?' said Leon. 'What is it? You sit stills. You be quiets. Now we watch.'

However young, she danced with tremulous invitation, a slow, yearning, graceful dance, the long fan feathers sweeping over her body in alternating curves, a dance that began from a crouching position and opened gradually upwards as she rose, inch by inch, a celestial bird, some as yet undiscovered hornbill of paradise, flying upwards towards the sun, towards the bright world where Bali Penyalong is Lord of the House.

'This is really something,' whispered James, holding his head in both hands, gazing at her. And then, perhaps remembering his professional self, his column inches, 'She *really, really* knows what she's doing.'

The two fans of the tail feathers of the Rhinoceros hornbill, at the end of her outstretched arms, joined above her head. She stood at her full height, little, curved, lissom, beautiful. We clapped and clapped.

And then, suddenly looking straight at us, giving us a small charge of our own internal electricity, a conger eel uncurling in the guts, she walked into the audience with every eye upon her and pulled Leon to his feet.

Leon's brown face grew browner and browner. He was blushing. He was suffusing, uncontrollably, with blood, and surprise, with fright and pride, with increasing vigour and overpowering lust.

She tied him, very slowly, into the helmet and the war-coat, lingering over every knot, staring steadily into his eyes, hanging the belt around his waist with both her hands, arranging the silver *parang* so that it hung neatly down the outside of his right thigh.

Leon, taller and darker than the Kenyah, and just as fit, stood like a warrior; and this was his reward, I realized. For Leon, conqueror of the river, as she must have heard, had proved his manhood and his spontaneous, natural courage as surely as if he had arrived at Nanga Sinyut with a severed head. In our eyes, and probably in theirs, he had done much better: he had saved one, and a particularly fine specimen, too, a Bald godhead rescued from a blow among the rocks.

Still fired with inspiration, his face growing even darker, he nodded to his little muse in lordly fashion as she returned to her seat. He then, I am sure, executed the finest dance of his life. To the frantic music of open combat, he somersaulted backwards; he cartwheeled from side to side; he cut heads like corn; he lunged and feinted and dodged behind his imaginary shield; he twisted and spun through the air faster than flying spears. For his new love, he topped whole armies. He moved with such energy that black-and-white banded wheels, images of hornbill feathers, arcs and lines, seemed to hang in the murk all around him, fading and appearing in the flicker of the lamp.

Finally, the music stopped and Leon, shiny with sweat and grasping, I assume, a bundle of heads, strode with them to the side of his beloved and dropped them in her lap. In the stunned, short pause before the clapping began I heard an odd noise. It was not a gecko. It was Leon's watch. It was as shaken and overexcited as he was. *Beeeep-beeeep-beeeep*, it said.

Leon, disrobed, momentarily speechless with exertion and wanting a rest, woke up Inghai with his foot. Ingy-Pingy, bleary but goodnatured, not at all sure where he was, did the kind of kung fu which a dormouse might do on arising from hibernation. He yawned and uncurled and stretched his arms and legs full out a bit, and then went back to sleep.

The formal gathering broke up into small groups, drinking and laughing and telling stories. The largest circle grew around James. The Kenyah sat at his feet in rings, listening to his bizarre tales of life in England. They studied his expressive face and his agitated gestures, laughing at the right moments, tingling, when required, at the voice from the Hammer House of Horror, just as if they knew where Rugeley was, or were connoisseurs of murder, or understood two words of what he said.

Maybe the *arak* and *tuak* were beginning to tell on me. My legs seemed to have contracted elephantiasis. It was difficult to focus. The longhouse pitched a bit, like an anchored canoe. Or maybe I was simply coming to the end of the longest day I ever hope to traverse.

As if from a long way off, I heard James issue a solemn warning to his audience:

> The Butcher bird, or Red-backed shrike
> Should not be trusted with your bike
> The pump and light he whips away
> And takes the spokes to spike his prey.

It was an entirely new, unpublished Fenton poem, I realized, dimly. But whatever it was, it was beyond me. And so were the Kenyah. I staggered, luckily, the right way off the verandah, through the correct *bilek* door, and found my patch of board. Through the wooden wall I could hear James singing songs, parcelling out the verses, teaching the Kenyah English. I fell asleep.

ISABEL ALLENDE · *Voices in My Ear*

NICHOLSON BAKER · *Playing Trombone*

LINDSEY BAREHAM · *The Little Book of Big Soups*

KAREN BLIXEN · *From the Ngong Hills*

DIRK BOGARDE · *Coming of Age*

ANTHONY BURGESS · *Childhood*

ANGELA CARTER · *Lizzie Borden*

CARLOS CASTANEDA · *The Sorcerer's Ring of Power*

ELIZABETH DAVID · *Peperonata and Other Italian Dishes*

RICHARD DAWKINS · *The Pocket Watchmaker*

GERALD DURRELL · *The Pageant of Fireflies*

RICHARD ELLMANN · *The Trial of Oscar Wilde*

EPICURUS · *Letter on Happiness*

MARIANNE FAITHFULL · *Year One*

KEITH FLOYD · *Hot and Spicy Floyd*

ALEXANDER FRATER · *Where the Dawn Comes Up Like Thunder*

ESTHER FREUD · *Meeting Bilal*

JOHN KENNETH GALBRAITH · *The Culture of Contentment*

ROB GRANT AND DOUG NAYLOR · *Scenes from the Dwarf*

ROBERT GRAVES · *The Gods of Olympus*

JANE GRIGSON · *Puddings*

SOPHIE GRIGSON · *From Sophie's Table*

KATHARINE HEPBURN · *Little Me*

SUSAN HILL · *The Badness Within Him*

ALAN HOLLINGHURST · *Adventures Underground*

BARRY HUMPHRIES · *Less is More Please*

HOWARD JACOBSON · *Expulsion from Paradise*

P. D. JAMES · *The Girl Who Loved Graveyards*

STEPHEN KING · *Umney's Last Case*

LAO TZU · *Tao Te Ching*

DAVID LEAVITT · *Chips Is Here*

READ MORE IN PENGUIN

For complete information about books available from Penguin and how to order them, please write to us at the appropriate address below. Please note that for copyright reasons the selection of books varies from country to country.

IN THE UNITED KINGDOM: Please write to *Dept. EP, Penguin Books Ltd, Bath Road, Harmondsworth, Middlesex UB7 0DA.*

IN THE UNITED STATES: Please write to *Consumer Sales, Penguin USA, P.O. Box 999, Dept. 17109, Bergenfield, New Jersey 07621-0120.* VISA and MasterCard holders call 1-800-253-6476 to order Penguin titles.

IN CANADA: Please write to *Penguin Books Canada Ltd, 10 Alcorn Avenue, Suite 300, Toronto, Ontario M4V 3B2.*

IN AUSTRALIA: Please write to *Penguin Books Australia Ltd, P.O. Box 257, Ringwood, Victoria 3134.*

IN NEW ZEALAND: Please write to *Penguin Books (NZ) Ltd, Private Bag 102902, North Shore Mail Centre, Auckland 10.*

IN INDIA: Please write to *Penguin Books India Pvt Ltd, 706 Eros Apartments, 56 Nehru Place, New Delhi 110 019.*

IN THE NETHERLANDS: Please write to *Penguin Books Netherlands bv, Postbus 3507, NL-1001 AH Amsterdam.*

IN GERMANY: Please write to *Penguin Books Deutschland GmbH, Metzlerstrasse 26, 60594 Frankfurt am Main.*

IN SPAIN: Please write to *Penguin Books S. A., Bravo Murillo 19, 1° B, 28015 Madrid.*

IN ITALY: Please write to *Penguin Italia s.r.l., Via Felice Casati 20, I-20124 Milano.*

IN FRANCE: Please write to *Penguin France S. A., 17 rue Lejeune, F-31000 Toulouse.*

IN JAPAN: Please write to *Penguin Books Japan, Ishikiribashi Building, 2-5-4, Suido, Bunkyo-ku, Tokyo 112.*

IN GREECE: Please write to *Penguin Hellas Ltd, Dimocritou 3, GR-106 71 Athens.*

IN SOUTH AFRICA: Please write to *Longman Penguin Southern Africa (Pty) Ltd, Private Bag X08, Bertsham 2013.*